# Viridian Glade

Cara Arnold

BookLeaf Publishing

India | USA | UK

Made with ❤ on the BookLeaf Publishing Platform
www.bookleafpub.in
www.bookleafpub.com

# Dedication

For Chuck, who occasionally believes in me

# Preface

Dear Reader,

Congratulations on picking up this book! Whether you're here by choice or some bizarre twist of fate, buckle up. You're in for a weird poetry ride. This is my first attempt to write anything in many years, so you get the good, the bad, and the strange.

If you spot a typo or two, just consider it a special feature.

Expect the unexpected. And remember, laughter is not only allowed but encouraged. Enjoy the book or don't, my feelings are not easily hurt. This book was written as part of a 21 days of poetry challenge for the first 21 days of 2025 so here are some first ramblings of the year.

Happy reading!

# Acknowledgements

With heartfelt gratitude, I would like to extend my sincerest thanks to those who support me in all my endeavors. To my husband, thank you for your endless encouragement, patience, and understanding. Your love inspires almost everything I do. To my friends and family, thank you for all the laughter and inspiration that you bring to my life. And to my wonderful dogs, thank you for your unconditional love, companionship, and the joy you bring to my life everyday. Your playful spirits are a constant reminder of the simple joy in my life. I love you all, Thank you.

# Night Fox

There once was a fox oh so sly,
Who gazed at the moon in the sky.
He'd prance and he'd leap,
While others would sleep,
Always looking for chickens nearby.

# Cozy

The snow falls gently outside the frosted pane of glass,
It skitters in the wind before finding its place in the
already white earth,
A cold winter land out there has started to amass,
But it is so nice and coxy here in front of the hearth.

Outside the sky is grey, the temperature frigid.
Inside by the fire my book pages are warm.
The frozen branches outside are all rigid,
On the edge of the roof the icicles do form.

I thank the ancestors for all their inventions,
My blanket so soft, my fireplace so reliable,
Staying inside covers all my intentions,
All these amenities make this all viable.

I snuggle and read about dragons and romance
I look out to the world to see a snowy hill scape
The smell of the fire in my nose, does its dance
My fireplace reading is my best escape

# Christmas Haiku

Puppy snores softly
Fireplace crackles gently
Santa is aflame

# Sparks of hope

Cold steel ceilings, floors, and walls
Loud metal steps as I run through the halls
Sparks fly from an open panel on my right
Repairs need to be done, but I need more light.

The darkness of space now leaks inside,
Power is low, the damage is wide.
Life support wont hold very much longer
The sadness begins, despair grows much stronger

Wind starts to blow and I know its the end
The ship starts to creak, the bridge starts to bend
One last look out the port- stars all abound
an endless night begins without any sound

# Ball

My pup has five tennis balls bright,
Which fills her heart up with delight.
She'll fetch and she'll play,
Till the dark end of day,
If you try to take one there will be a fight.

# Teaching Acrostic

In the classroom I spend my days

Wisdom shared in countless ways.
Always giving, guiding, showing,
Nurturing young minds, forever growing.
The questions they ask, well they never end,

To their emotions we often must tend.
Outside time is the best time of day,

Getting to finally go out an play.
Obligations never do cease,

Hoping for just one moment's peace.
Oh my, what is that on the floor?
My days never-ending, but never a bore.
Eagerly tomorrow we do it once more.

# Globe

There once was a globe that could spin,
Showing lands from Beijing to Berlin
From deserts to snow,
It put on a show,
Much to flat-earthers' eternal chagrin.

# Stay calm

Once in a quiet timbered grove, a little old bald man was on his way through to the cove. He stumbled upon a snow-white bear, Both startled by the other's stare.

Their eyes locked in a frozen fright, Each poised to flee into the night. The man, with a cane and ancient knees, The bear, with muscles strong enough to climb trees.

A heartbeat passed, then two, then three, In silence born of mutual plea. "Let's part, old friend," the man did think, The bear agreed with just a blink.

And so they turned, both homeward bound, With new respect they both had found. The man returned to his old rocking chair, The bear, to its cold icy lair.

In dreams, they'd laugh at that strange sight: A bald old man and bear in fright. Two souls that met but dared not stay, Each found their peace and walked away.

# Popcorn, Peanuts, and Pistachios

The smell of the popcorn so perfectly wafts, shouts from
concession can be heard in the lofts.
Peanut shells are crunching in the aisles and the seats,
while performers show off their beautiful feats.

In the heart of the circus, under the big top, A clown on
a unicycle, a sight that just won't stop.
His suit's a kaleidoscope, his shoes way too large, they
might be compared to the size of a barge.

The crowd erupts in laughter and and also with cheer,
For the clown and chimpanzee, who don't know any fear.
Through fire and hoops, on that one single wheel, Their
bond is astounding, quite a heartwarming deal.

But beneath the paint, a story is told, Of dreams and
travels, of tales of old.
The clown's bright painted smile so unmistakably wide,
Together they journey through life side by side.

The clown honks his horn, the shows almost done, he
gets in one last gag, a flower pops out from his gun
The kids all giggle at a dog shaped balloon, and they all
hope that they can visit the circus again soon.

# Evening

The day starts to whisper goodbye,
The colors inherit the sky
They flow and they bloom
But the darkness will loom
So enjoy natures sweet lullaby

# Viridian Glade

In a glade where green meets sky, serene, Where human footprints have never been seen, Nature thrives in harmonious play, In this emerald haven, so far away.
The ancient trees, their branches entwined, Shelter secrets, ancient and kind. Leaves whisper tales of ages past, In a world where time moves slow, never fast.
Birds serenade with songs of cheer, Deer graze quietly, always without fear. Butterflies dance on a gentle breeze, In this veridian glade, a life full of ease.
Streams weave throughout with a silvery grace, Reflecting the sun's warm happy embrace. Flowers bloom in a riot of hues, In this untouched paradise, such wonderful views.
Foxes play in the dappled light, Owls take flight in the soft twilight. Creatures big and small find their place, In this glade, a sanctuary, a sacred space.
Love abounds in every creature's heart, In this wild symphony, each plays a part. A world so pure, so beautifully made, An Eden untouched, this viridian glade.

# Hopes

I dream of places far and wide, Of sandy beaches, and ocean tides. I long to see the Eiffel Tower, But my bank account holds all the power.
I picture Venice, a gondola ride, But can not even afford a travel guide. Ice hotels in Norway, Northern lights shine by night, But with my savings? Barely enough for a flight.
I plan my trips with utmost care, But quickly realize, I'm going nowhere. So I just sit on the internet dreaming of someday when I can figure out someway to pay.
For now, my passport gathers dust, While my wanderlust turns to mild distrust. But someday soon, I'll pack my case, And set off for far lands with a smile on my face.

# Midnight Flight

In shadows deep, where secrets lie, a fierce golden
dragon begins to fly
With scales that shimmer in the night sky, she takes to
flight way up high.
Eyes like embers burning bright, she soars above with all
her might
those below are full of fright, as she flaps and glides
throughout the night
She searches for treasures to add to her keep, but gets
distracted by tasty sheep
She swoops down to grab some as they start to leap, she
is so quick and her teeth sink so deep.
As moonlight glints off of her golden scales, she flies
over the coast gliding on gales,
Below her there surfaces a pod of whales, then she spots
the large black sails
She knows there will be treasure below their deck, her
wings start to lower and so does her neck
Lucky for her the old ship is low-tech, she swoops down
quickly creating a wreck

Wood cracks and splinters and even does spray, she
attacked it as if it was just normal prey,
She grabs all the gold and and then goes on her way,
returning to her cave just before day.

# Haiku

Umbrella with stripes
Large red beach towel, white dog
But where is Waldo?

# Painting

As I bundle up real nice and snug,
I think that I'll paint a bright ladybug.
By a happy little tree,
It's as cute as can be,
Just don't drink out of the paint water mug.

# Atari

In a world of pixels, blocky and bright,
Stood the Atari 2600, a gamer's delight.
With a joystick in hand and a CRT glow,
Players ventured to realms, learning what we now know.
From Adventure to Keystone Kaper's chase,
Porky's and Pitfall, each game had its place.
In basements all across world, the console reigned,
A revolution in gaming, forever ingrained.
Beeps and boops, the soundtrack of my youth,
The fun it conveyed is not at all hard to sleuth.
With simple graphics and gameplay pure,
The Atari's magic, an age to endure.
With colorful cartridges, we'd swap and we'd share,
Creating our memories, beyond compare.
A relic now, but oh, what a start,
In the world of gaming, it played a big part.
Here's to the 2600, raise a tapper beer,
A classic in gaming, year after year.

# Harsh World

This wondrous world is clouded with choices, We wind
and turn, led by many voices. Whom should we follow,
whom should we trust? As we grow older, we do what
we must.

Along comes an ally, a small, fluffy friend, They show us
the path with a heart they extend. They love without
limit, they guide every day, Teaching us to follow as they
lead the way.

Their life gets extinguished before we comprehend, We
try to keep going alone once again. The lesson you
taught us, most wonderful friend, Do not give up like
you would have back then.

Honor their memory, run in the sun, Eat lots of snacks,
and don't come undone. Find another companion, don't
give into grief, Keep your head up, we know that time is
a thief.

Rescue a new friend, show them all the compassion, Give them your whole heart, there is no need to ration. It is what they would want you to do, Continue with your life, and love someone new.

# New Outfit

Boomer is quite a sassy dog, and this is her monologue:

With a sigh and a huff, I sit quite still,
As I am put in clothes against my will.
A sweater, a hat! I have had enough of that!
I look in the mirror with a pout,
Wishing I could just run about.
They say I am cute,
but I don't give a hoot
Take this off of me now,
it's time to say ciao
So mad I could spit,
take off this outfit
Do as you are told,
oh wait, now I am cold

# Books on a shelf

There can never be too many books,
Hardback, paperback, kindle, or nooks.
They will patiently wait for their turn,
If you own them then they never will burn,
But my whole life they can wait,
with the worlds they create,
my to be read list will only grow longer
my need to read will only grow stronger,
some day I can retire and read
I will have all the time that I need
This is a lie I tell myself
As I continue to fill up my shelf

# My Friend

I truly do wish you all of the best,
our friendship has passed the whole test
I will walk right there by your side,
we can take turns being the guide
Tell me all your troubles, get them off of your chest
even the things that are hard to digest,
we can face them together, not hide
we can sit until the pain does subside
We'll walk again once we are no longer distressed,
In both of our futures and happiness let's invest.

# Halcyon

*I arrived at the lift for the Starcruiser by noon,*
*Onboard, a galaxy before my eyes did bloom.*
*The atrium dazzled, such a wondrous sight,*
*Never had I seen such beauty, its a wonderous delight.*
*Being inside a spaceship, a dream of mine,*
*To the Crown of Corellia, to feast and to dine.*
*A mysterious man spoke of an antic ahead,*
*Excitement surged, my heart swiftly sped.*
*Then there was a call, we all headed to muster,*
*"Cresh!" we shouted, as we sat in our cluster.*
*Raithe appeared, with a plan in his hand,*
*Distract the lawmen, trap them as planned.*
*Zooming off to adventures, our spirits soared high,*
*A rebel lieutenant arrived, yes our own furry spy.*
*In the dance of diversion, we moved as one,*
*Avoiding pursuers, it was so much fun.*
*Our quest led us to the bridge of the ship,*
*Sneaking past the guards we gave them the slip.*
*The trip flew by, a blur of delight,*
*Sadly, it's now a memory, fading from sight.*

www.ingramcontent.com/pod-product-compliance
Lightning Source LLC
LaVergne TN
LVHW021345200726
843509LV00014B/2670